KEVIN TUTT & MICHAEL DAGGS

TRAPPED!

ESCAPING THE COMFORT OF COMPLACENCY

You have the **POWER** to make a difference
MAKE EVERY MOMENT COUNT

TRAPPED! Escaping the Comfort of Complacency
published by **Kouba Graphics Inc., USA,** www.koubagraphics.com

No part of this book may be reproduced or transmitted in any form or by any means, electronic or mechanical, including scanning, photocopying, recording, or by any information storage and retrieval system, without permission in writing from Tutt & Daggs. Inquiries can be made via the www.tuttdaggs.com website.

Printed in the United States of America, 2015.
ISBN 978-1-938577-02-4

Layout and design by Kouba Graphics, Inc.
Consulting and editing by On-time Writing.

10 9 8 7 6 5 4 3 2 1

DEDICATION

To our wives Caroline Daggs and Marci Tutt, who have been our greatest supporters and continuously encourage us to keep dreaming.

To our kids, who inspire and amaze us with the things they say and do and the pride we feel for their accomplishments and life lessons learned.

To our parents, who started us on our original adventure and have always expected great things from us and for their personal testament that complacency is not an option.

To our brothers and sister, nieces and nephews, aunts and uncles, cousins and extended family that are woven into the fabric of our stories and our daily lives.

We are truly blessed by all of you!

TRAPPED!

Escaping the Comfort of Complacency

TABLE OF CONTENTS

Introduction
By Kevin Tutt

Over the past several years, Michael and I have visited with several hundred presidents, CEOs and business leaders as we prepare to provide staff training for their workforce. Each time we enter into a new relationship with a company or organization, they want to share "their story," because they are sure their story is different from other organizations. "Their story" goes something like this: I just wish our employees would take more ownership or be more committed to their careers. I want them to be self-starters, motivated, proactive, take the initiative, take responsibility, hold themselves and others accountable, run this company as if it were their own, be more productive, be more efficient . . . . And the list goes on. As much as everyone wants their story to be unique and different, the fact is, it is not. Everyone's story is similar.

As Mike and I prepared for training year after year, it became clear that these organizational leaders are battling employee complacency. Complacency is the trap that lures each of us into a "good enough" or "that'll do" mentality. You don't mean any harm by it and you're not trying to be lazy. We totally understand that "good enough" and "that'll do" are often the best results that can be attained at a given time. The trap of complacency, however, is becoming comfortable with these results. Because they worked once, why not just set that as the new standard?

It is human nature to try to make things easier, more routine or, as the book title suggests, more comfortable. We see comfort as a good thing, and in and of itself, it is. However, when we become comfortable with what seems to be good enough, we lose the drive that leaders want in individuals. There is no more passion, motivation, excitement, ownership, accountability or initiative. The fact is, we become dormant and find ourselves simply going through the motions of life, in our careers, families and personal life. We begin to complain that it is the fault of others around us—my job, my boss, my spouse, my kids, my friends—when the reality is that we have simply stepped squarely into the trap of complacency.

This book will address seven key areas to help free you from complacency and challenge you to rekindle your passion and desire for success. You will find that some of life's most satisfying journeys are the result of a little, or maybe even a lot of, discomfort. Mike and I often reflect on some of our life activities like hiking, snow skiing, kayaking, whitewater rafting, camping, coaching, speaking, training, fishing and hunting. The truth is the most satisfying of each of these is completing the journey. Getting to the summit of a mountain or the top of a snow hill is awesome, but it is not comfortable. It is hard work and it would be so much easier to sit in the lodge and drink a mocha cappuccino and ask others how it was at the top. But that's the trap! Our hope is that you will take the time to truly reflect on your career and life and answer the questions following each chapter with absolute honesty. This book is not meant to be shared with others but instead should be a reminder to you as you look back regularly at your notes. At the end of reading it, Mike and I hope you are truly free from the trap of complacency and live a life filled with greatness!

CHAPTER 1

Change Your Course.
By Michael Daggs

Change Your Course.

In January 1988, Michael Jackson popularized a song written by Glen Ballard and Siedan Garret called "Man in the Mirror." The song is a call to a straightforward commitment to personally examine oneself as the starting point for greater success. We cannot avoid complacency and become who we were meant to be without the mirror. Successful people constantly hold up a mirror to their lives.

The great and yet troubling thing about the mirror is that it shows no favoritism, keeps no secrets and does not hide blemishes. It simply reflects the truth. It tells the story of what stands before it. High performers recognize this and constantly ask the key questions: What am I doing? How am I doing? Why am I doing these things?

Understanding the value of the mirror and the willingness to use it is the number one key. You must look in the mirror! Complacency and comfort do not see the need nor have the desire to look in the mirror.

In the summer of 1999, I found my professional life in a transition period. I was leaving my current employment and moving four hours south to work for a different organization. It was an emotional time for me because some of my professional relationships had turned into very strong friendships. My wife, Caroline, and I decided that she would travel ahead of me by a few days to visit with her family in the Dallas area. Following a going-away party a few days later, I planned to meet up with her and continue our travel together.

On July 8, 1999, I began the journey. Leaving from Eastland, Texas, I would travel I-20 approximately three hours to meet with my wife. The previous night, a significant rain system had drenched the entire route I was scheduled to take. I left early that morning, ensuring that I allowed adequate time to travel so I would not have to hurry in the weather conditions.

Everything was going smoothly as I crested a hill in Weatherford, Texas. Descending the hill, I was in the process of passing an 18-wheel truck. When we got to the bottom of the hill, the big rig and my Mazda pickup hit the beginning of a small bridge at the exact same time. At that moment, the truck caused an enormous amount of water to shoot onto my windshield and before my windshield wipers could clear the water, I began to hydroplane across the bridge. In one heartbeat, my truck had turned 180 degrees and then was facing the cars that were once behind me. Cars were now directly in front of me and I began to cross the bridge backwards. I remember holding the steering wheel thinking that this was the end of my life. Even though it all happened very fast, I remember thinking about my survival options and they were all bad. To my left was the truck and to my right was the bridge. So I hung on, completely out of control, waiting for the worst. Somehow, while navigating backward across the bridge, I avoided going under the semi or over the bridge. However, I was quickly traveling toward the median, heading directly for the oncoming traffic.

At mile marker 402, a row of wooden posts held a guardrail, preventing traffic from crossing the median. The last post in that guardrail is the one that saved my life. The back right part of the bumper of my car hit that last post, preventing me from going straight into oncoming traffic, but it also turned me sideways, causing me to roll seven times down the hill of the median.

When the rolling stopped and it was obvious that I had survived, I immediately began to survey my body for injury. Miraculously, I had no physical injuries. I didn't have a broken bone, a scratch, a seat belt burn, nothing. After I realized that I was unhurt, I began to clue in to my surroundings.

I noticed that the radio was still on. Ironically, the song playing in that moment was "Another One Bites the Dust" by Queen. Somehow I still had enough sense of humor to appreciate the moment.

Though I was alive and my body was undamaged, the inside of the truck was a different story. The passenger side door was mashed toward the driver side, leaving the passenger seat virtually destroyed. The extended cab was crushed toward the front of the cab. The front of the cab was completely unrecognizable, as the bumper was about four feet from my face, inside of the busted windshield.

I pulled myself out of what once was the passenger side window and began to survey the scene from outside of the truck. At this point, many people had pulled over and were rushing to my aid. I could also hear sirens quickly approaching, but one thing resonated in that moment more than anything else. It was obvious that only someone about my size, sitting in the exact place that I was sitting (in the driver's seat) would have survived that wreck.

7

At that moment I understood death can be a heartbeat away. But I had not died. I had been given the opportunity to be a better husband, father, son, employee—the list goes on and on. Was I who I wanted to be? You only live once. I wanted to live what life I had left differently, not simply going through the motions. I wanted to live life to its fullest. I didn't want to be lazy. Whatever I believed I was supposed to do with my life, I wanted to be great. I wanted to do my best. I made a decision in the pouring rain on I-20 that I must get free from the comfort of complacency and live life daily with a purpose.

A Call to Look at Yourself

Below is a transcript of a conversation between a U.S. naval ship and Canadian authorities off the coast of Newfoundland.

Americans: "Please divert your course 15 degrees to the north to avoid collision."

Canadians: "Recommend you divert YOUR course 15 degrees to the south to avoid a collision."

Americans: "This is the captain of a U.S. Navy ship. I say again, divert YOUR course."

Canadians: "No, I say again, you divert YOUR course."

Americans: "This is the Aircraft Carrier USS Abraham Lincoln, the second largest ship in the United States' Atlantic Fleet. We are accompanied by three destroyers, three cruisers and numerous support vessels. I demand that you change your course 15 degrees north. That's one-five degrees north, or counter measures will be undertaken to ensure the safety of this ship."

Canadians: "This is a lighthouse. It's your call."

A huge challenge we face is wanting others or situations to change. It is often easier to demand that they change rather than that we change. To free yourself from the complacency trap, you have to begin by examining yourself.

Where Are You?

You don't have to have a life-changing event to realize you need to change your course. Sometimes we need to take a look at our lives and careers from an outside perspective. Simply look in the mirror and ask the tough questions, "Have I stumbled into the trap of complacency and do I need to change my course?"

Change Your Course.

Have you become comfortable in the complacency trap?

_____

_____

_____

Identify areas in your life that have become complacent:

_____

_____

_____

How could they be different? _____

_____

_____

_____

CHAPTER 2

You've Got to Want This.

By Kevin Tutt

You've Got to Want This.

After taking a close look in the mirror and evaluating who you are, the next key is to identify your strengths and what you do best.

I like speaking to people. As a matter of fact, I try to make conversation any time I have a chance. One of the things I've noticed, especially when I try to strike up a conversation in the workplace, is the number of people who are trapped in their circumstances. What I mean by this is they have become numb to their ability to make a difference and instead have chosen a path of doom and gloom.

Some of the most common responses I get from my question, "How are you?" include: "Could be better." "I've had better days." "It feels like a Monday all over again." "You don't want to know." "Just a couple more hours until quitting time." "Ask me around 5 o'clock." "It's almost Friday." "It's beer-30 somewhere." "I'm surviving, just another day." "Another day, another dollar." "I'm here." But the most common response is a blank stare that says to me, "Get out of my space."

These reactions tell me that a significant number of people go through life every day not really doing what they like or what they are good at.

For the past several years, my brother and I have taken our families on a great fall adventure to Dallas, where we do back-to-school shopping at the Grapevine Mills Mall. It is no regular mall. It is a mega mall that promises to deliver a mega experience. As you might imagine, as we headed east from Abilene toward Dallas, my wife and two daughters were excited and happy, happy, happy. They cranked up the peppy, praise music for our three-hour trip and the atmosphere was pure jubilation. To say that my family was passionate about this trip would be an understatement. However, I was not so elated. It did make me smile to see my troops excited about something, but I have to admit this was not the kind of thing that I lived for. I would describe my engagement level as "going through the motions" at best.

On our last trip, our convoy arrived at the mall parking lot just minutes before the stores opened. I could tell everyone was ready to storm the field. My wife, Marci, had a little extra hop in her step as she trotted across the parking lot, "stiff-arming" traffic and making her way into the building. My daughters, Kelsey and Karson, followed with a walk-run-skip maneuver. I heard something like, "We'll holler at ya later," as they waved goodbye to me. At this point, my brother Cleve, who had parked beside me, and I watched our two families of girls vanish into the abyss.

While walking into the mall, I looked down at my watch and, like Chevy Chase in a *Vacation* moment, I say, "We did it! We got here at the exact time they open."

I'm no rookie to this adventure. I was aware that it was going to be a long day, so I had done everything to set myself up for success. I had worn my most comfortable running shoes, my favorite cargo shorts and my "Life Is Good" t-shirt to help with my attitude.

Even in my most comfortable attire, after about 30 minutes of strolling around the mall I began to get a dull ache in the back of my neck. My back began to tighten up. The arches of my feet began to hurt. My sciatic nerve began to throb down my leg, and I found myself limping. My fatigue continued to contribute to my disengagement as the day rolled on. Before I knew it, I was strictly in survival mode. Another contributor to my disengagement was that it was Saturday, in the fall. That meant college football game day. Hundreds of games were taking place all over America, and I was limping around a shopping mall.

To set myself up for success this particular day, I had sent Kelsey, Karson and Marci shopping together. I thought it was perfect. I would have no real role in the day except to carry the bags out to the car when I received the call. I am an optimist.

Around 3:30 p.m., I got a call from Kelsey. Before I answered I saw that it was her number and I immediately thought, "We're done! They've found everything and are ready to go!" In actuality, the call went more like this:

Me: "Hey Kels, What's up?"

Kelsey: "Hey, Dad, we're down at the Buckle and mom wants you to come look at some jeans I'm trying on."

I was fully aware that this call from my daughter was code from my wife to get down there and tell her no.

Me: "Come on, Kelsey. I don't want to walk down there and look at pants. I'm in sector 43. It'll take me 20 minutes to walk all the way down there."

Kelsey: "Please dad, I've been looking for these everywhere and I finally found my size."

If you have teenage girls you know the whining of this conversation. Still optimistically trying to stay committed to the day, I said, "Ok, I'll limp that way." As I walked into the Buckle, I saw Kelsey was all smiles, waiting for me to see the elusive jeans she had finally found. As she stood there appearing to be hopped up on a five-hour energy drink, I caught a glimpse of my wife, Marci, and I recognized her ever so subtle eye and head gestures communicate, "No way!"

I turned to Kelsey and tried to communicate on her level.

Me: "Those are cute. Let me see the back. Ok, now raise your shirt a little. (Pause) Well, Kels, I have a question."

Kelsey: "Ok."

Me: "Are those going to be your plumbing pants?"

Kelsey: "What?"

Me: "I'm not sure if you're aware of this but when you raise your shirt up or bend over, your crack shows!"

Kelsey: "Dad, they're called low rise and my crack won't show when I wear them with a longer shirt."

Me: "You're right a longer shirt would be better, but there's a chance you won't always have a longer shirt, so those jeans aren't going to cut it."

Being a typical teenage girl, she went into panic mode.

Kelsey: "Wait, don't leave! You gotta see these others."

She zipped into the dressing room and quickly reappeared with another pair of jeans. This pair of jeans looked like it was dug out of the rag box after it had been used to clean up several acid and bleach spills. She informed me that the official adjective for these jeans was "distressed." I reached over to take a look at the price tag and I became distressed. $149! I looked at Kelsey.

Me: "Kelsey, look at me. I have a full-time job. I stand in front of thousands of people a year and nothing I wear costs $149. And you want me to spend that on a pair of torn up jeans?"

I didn't even wait for an answer. I exited the store and continued my downward spiral toward disengagement.

We finally survived the day and around 5:30 p.m., we were headed to the car, bags in tow. I was still limping. The look of exhaustion was on everyone's faces. This day was not over, however. Backing out of my parking space, I drove literally half a mile across the street and parked the car. We exited the car, and as we started toward a different building, suddenly my limp was cured. I began walking with the excitement and energy that my girls started the day with. I was headed into the paradise known as Outdoor World Bass Pro Shop.

It was like a miracle cure. I honestly hadn't been faking pain all day. I really did hurt. But I knew that if I could just get to the threshold of Bass Pro Shop it would be, whoosh, I'm cured. No pain!

I turned to check on my family and, you got it, they were all limping. They asked, "Can we just go check into the hotel?" My response was, "No." They needed to feel my pain of walking around the mall for hours, waiting to leave. Here was the strange thing. I can honestly stay in Bass Pro Shop for hours, maybe even days, looking at things. I had no intention of buying anything. I just love looking at all the cool stuff there. Cleve and I were like kids in a candy store while our girls headed over to Uncle Bucks to have a snack and rest.

Yagottawanta

I am a positive individual. I work hard to try to make things better in whatever it is that I'm doing. In most of our workshops and keynotes, Michael and I discuss three levels of engagement or, in other terms, one's level of commitment. Several research projects have identified commitment levels, but each of them, in various terms, comes down to these three: committed, enduring and destructive. We most often refer to them, as identified by the Gallup Organization, as engaged, disengaged and actively disengaged.

You see, when I'm at Grapevine Mills Mall I am disengaged, in what we call the complacency trap. I am just going through the motions, trying to survive. My wife and daughters are engaged and to some degree, hyper-engaged. They are completely committed to the task of shopping and getting things ready for the fall semester. But then in a 5 to 10 minute switch, as we drive across the parking lot to Outdoor World Bass Pro Shop, suddenly I am transformed from a disengaged tag-along to a passionate shopper, freed from complacency and pain and totally focused and committed. My family, on the other hand, immediately transitions to tired, hurting, exhausted and in survival mode. They have stepped into the complacency trap.

What causes the same people to slide from one state to the next in a matter of minutes and, in many cases, seconds? I believe that the answer is interest. When I'm at the mall, I am not interested. My family, however, is very interested. It motivates them to stay committed and they have the energy to maintain their engagement. When I walk into Bass Pro Shop, I feel the same. I become completely interested in what I'm doing. I have energy and stamina to stay committed to the task of browsing a huge store.

Please understand this! If you want to be better, move forward or improve upon a situation, then realize improvement will not happen on its own. The fact is yagottawanta. It's important you don't misunderstand what I'm saying. I didn't say things wouldn't change. Things change whether we want them to or not. Remaining in the complacency trap simply limits your ability to influence change.

Interest leads to commitment, and commitment leads to passion. Lots of players are interested in playing in the NFL and they make it because of their commitment. But the most successful players are those who combine that commitment with passion. Once they lose their interest in the game, it's not long before they are trapped trying to do just enough and soon they're done.

What Do You Want?

What are you naturally drawn to? _____

_____

_____

_____

_____

What things are stealing your interest? _____

_____

_____

_____

_____

What are you committed to? _____

_____

_____

_____

_____

What are you passionate about? _____

_____

_____

_____

_____

What are you best at? _____

_____

_____

_____

What do you enjoy doing? _____

_____

_____

_____

_____

CHAPTER 3

Get a Fresh Perspective.
By Michael Daggs

GET A FRESH PERSPECTIVE.

How we interpret what happens to us and around us has tremendous influence in our lives. Often we simply see difficult times as unfortunate circumstances rather than the unseen opportunities they could be. We become trapped, held captive, by the situations we find ourselves in. Once again we may have never agreed to handle our circumstances the way we are but we have become comfortable and no one seems to expect more or anything different. It is simply easier to see things as they appear rather than how they could be different. As a result we remain in the grip of complacency when the opportunity for greatness is within our grasp.

I was blessed to have the opportunity to play college football. I was even more blessed to play for the Hardin-Simmons Athletic Hall of Fame coach, Jimmie Keeling, at a great institution called Hardin-Simmons University. I have many great memories of that time but one stands out over the rest.

It was a game day Saturday in the fall and I was hurrying to the charter bus that was waiting for us outside the field house. Hurrying was a way of life in those days because of a thing called "Keeling time." Keeling time was really a simple concept. It did not matter what time the rest of the world was going by, you needed to subtract about five minutes to be on Keeling time. If you showed up at the right time, then there was a good chance you were late. You did not want to be late.

Well, I was close to being late that morning as I boarded the charter bus. Immediately, I knew I should have been a little earlier. As I scanned the seat options, I was disappointed to discover that I was the last athlete to board and there was only one seat available. Which seat was it? No, it was not the seat next to coach Keeling, but the one directly behind him. Let's be honest here. Was coach Keeling a great coach? Yes. Did I want to sit that close to him? No. I was thankful this would be a rather short trip and there would be few opportunities for us to communicate. Or so I thought.

As the journey began I quickly pulled out my Walkman with the foam earphones and the mix tape I had dubbed the night before. (I just alienated half the readers with that last statement. Younger readers probably have no idea what a Walkman is or what dubbing a tape means. But the rest of you know what I'm referring to.)

The trip flew by with little interruption and much thought about our opponent. That was until we arrived on the outskirts of the town where the university that we were playing was located. As I remember, we had to navigate only one traffic light on the way to the stadium and we had just come to a stop at it. The stop signaled to everyone that we were just moments away from the stadium. It was only natural to look around our surroundings while we were sitting there. To my surprise, there appeared to be a large welcoming party congregating in the parking lot adjacent to the traffic light. There must have been around 500 people standing there. They were definitely excited as they yelled and jeered in our direction. Only it quickly became obvious that they were not hollering for us but at us. These people were fans of our opponent.

Suddenly, like they had planned the moment, every single person in the crowd of 500 lifted an arm in the air and then immediately put up the middle finger. Now, I've seen a few of those fingers pointed in my direction over the years, but I had never seen quite that many middle fingers in the air at one time. As one might imagine, the guys on my bus began standing up, looking out that side of the bus and, to put it mildly, did not receive that middle finger message very well.

Then it dawned on me that the hall-of-famer was sitting directly in front of me. I needed to see how he was going to handle this situation. He was always teaching us players about life lessons and the proper way to handle adversity. Now the time had come for that to be tested.

I took my attention off of the 500 middle fingers and looked at him. I'll never forget the look on his face as he digested the site before him. Keeling's face had tensed up as he stared right through them. I remember thinking that I would do about anything in that moment just to know what he was thinking. The traffic light changed from red to green and the bus began to leave the scene behind.

As the crowd faded in the rearview, the hall of fame coach turned around, looked me straight in the eyes, pointed his index finger directly at me and motioned me in for a closer conversation. Here it was! This was the moment that I had waited for! I cautiously moved toward him and waited with bated breath. Coach Keeling said, "Michael Daggs," pointing back toward their general direction, "They think we're number 1!"

This caught me completely off guard. I quickly turned to take another look and make sure I had seen the gesture correctly. Then my teammates and I began to laugh and a few even asked if coach knew what that meant. Following the statement, he turned around as if nothing ever happened. It was as if he never gave it another thought, creating another hall-of-fame Keeling moment.

A Fresh Perspective

Fifty college football players are all looking at the exact same thing as our coach. And what was done as a gesture to distract us and change our focus was certainly working. Then, in a spilt second, someone looking at the same thing we are chooses a different perspective and releases our laughter and instantly redirects our focus back to what is important. We were victorious against our opponent that day, but that is not the point here. Sometimes beyond our control, life is just not fair. Coach Keeling knew exactly what the crowd meant. He simply chose to look at the situation differently. Things happen that we do not plan on, see coming or ask for.

The lesson learned that day is that no matter what happens to you or the life circumstances that you are presented with, you possess the ability to choose how you will look at things. It's the power of perspective. The things that have the potential to wound us and hold us back also have the potential to grow us and set us free if we choose a perspective that gives us that opportunity.

Often we allow our circumstances to dictate our path. We find ourselves trapped where we are, no longer changing our perspective. Just like my teammates, we believe there is only one way to react, rather than seeing things differently and redirecting our focus on making things better.

You Walk, I Roll.

This change in perspective is exactly how one or our business partners lives his life daily. On March 11, 2005, Tyson Dever was preparing to turn left into his girlfriend's subdivision. It was their junior year at Texas State University and he was picking her up to head to South Padre Island for spring break. As Tyson sat in his convertible Corvette waiting for oncoming traffic to clear, he noticed a pickup behind him suddenly speed around him on the right shoulder. As he glanced up into his rearview mirror he realized why the pickup had taken off. Within seconds Tyson's car was hit by a fully loaded concrete truck that rolled over his car and pushed Tyson into oncoming traffic where he was then struck by another vehicle. His Corvette was a mangled mess and caught on fire. Bystanders were able to rescue him by shielding the flames with the car door that had been knocked loose and dragging him from the wreckage. Tyson suffered a major injury that morning that left him paralyzed from the waist down.

Tyson shares his story regularly as he speaks to students and organizations about overcoming obstacles. He shares the fact that some of his first words to his mother while in recovery, just minutes after finding out he would be in a wheelchair, were, "Well, I guess I'll have to learn to play wheelchair basketball." Tyson has chosen to change his perspective on everything in life. Doctors told him it would be difficult to ever hunt or fish again. They were right! It is more difficult getting into a deer blind or putting a bass boat onto the lake. But Tyson will tell you that the only difference between your life and his is this: "You walk, I roll."

Change the way you look at things, and things you look at will begin to change.

This chapter is in no way intended to gloss over or ignore circumstances that have happened or are currently happening to you. Hurt, anger, pain and grief are all real and justifiable emotions. The one common denominator in the countless stories we have heard and read about changing perspective is energy. In every case, the individuals chose to direct their energy toward making a positive impact.

What circumstances are you currently dealing with that you believe to be a trap? _____

_____

_____

_____

What situation (project, relationship, career, etc.) in your life needs a new perspective? _____

_____

_____

_____

Where is your energy spent in regard to the situation?

_____

_____

_____

Where can energy be redirected to have a positive impact?

_____

_____

_____

CHAPTER 4

Where You Are
Is Your Opportunity.

By Michael Daggs

WHERE YOU ARE
IS YOUR OPPORTUNITY.

Where you currently find yourself, right now, is where you should be making a difference. The trap of complacency is in thinking that you'll be different when you get a degree, get the right job, meet the right person, get the promotion or get the respect you deserve. The truth is, here and now is what you've got to work with.

The comfort of this trap is convincing yourself that "now is not my time." Let's face it. Doing nothing is much easier than making a difference in your life and lives of those around you. By convincing ourselves that no one cares, it's not important, I'll look foolish, nobody else does this, I'm a nobody, I have no influence, we stay trapped in the comfort zone. You can tell yourself, "The comfort zone doesn't feel great, but it's what I know and I can live with it." These are lies. You have the opportunity to influence, change and affect lives positively every single day. Enjoy this chapter and begin thinking about who you are and what you influence.

Somewhere along my travels, I have convinced myself that if I am going to eat fast food, then Arby's is at least a healthier fast food option. There is something about a market fresh sandwich, curly fries and a jamocha milkshake that just feels healthier.

About 10 years ago, one of my good friends and I decided to grab some food at an Arby's that we were conveniently passing by. It was about two o'clock on a Saturday afternoon and we were happy to see that no one else was in the drive-thru line. We assumed our experience would be a quick one. Boy, we were wrong.

As we pulled up to the speaker box and display, we were welcomed with the standard fast food greeting, "Welcome to Arby's. What can I get for you today?" As I recall, that was the last standard thing that happened during the encounter. I started the order by shouting into the speaker, "I'll take a market fresh sandwich, curly fries and a jamocha milkshake." The young lady on the other end of this speaker line responded in a way that I had never heard before. In a very high-pitched, Minnie Mouse squeaky voice, she said, "That's going to be one of the best sandwiches you'll ever eat. We are making that fresh for you right now!"

My friend and I were a little caught off guard by the response and chuckled. My friend gathered himself and began to place his order. Again, the high-pitched, Minnie Mouse voice came back to us with, "That's going to be one of the best sandwiches you'll ever eat. We are making that fresh for you right now." We could not help it. We began to laugh uncontrollably. We quickly tried to gain our composure as we approached the window where we would encounter the lady and our food.

We had no idea what was waiting around the turn. In all my journeys and fast food experiences, I was about to encounter a first. As we navigated the turn, I'll never forget what I saw. There was a young lady with a frizzy perm, red lipstick and a proud smile. But that's not all. She had grabbed underneath the top part of the drive-thru window and was leaning completely out, looking at us with her index finger pointing in our direction. As I was making my own observation, my friend finally saw what I already noticed and brought the car to a complete stop 20 feet from the window. He tried to hide his face under the dashboard and erupted into laughter. I could not stand the awkwardness of the lady hanging out of the drive-thru window staring at me in a car parked too far away, while my friend was ducking in the car. To avoid more awkwardness, I decided to duck, too, and we began to have a conversation under the dash. I looked at my friend and the following conversations took place.

Me: "What are you doing?"

Friend: "Man, there is no way I can go up there."

Me: "What do you mean you can't go up there?"

Friend: "Did you see her hanging out the window?"

I finally decided to come up from under the dash, trying to figure out a solution. The young lady was still as committed as ever. I looked in the rear view mirror hoping that we could reverse out of the awkward moment. Unfortunately, two cars were waiting behind us. So we ducked our heads back under the dash to devise another plan.

Me: "We have two options here. We can gas this thing and get out of here or we can go up there and embrace the awkwardness."

Of course, my friend was all too aware that I was looking forward to this impending encounter and knew that I was always on the lookout for people that behave differently and situations that would make for a good story.

Friend: "Ok, I'll go up there but whatever happens, don't embarrass me."

Me: "Fair enough."

We sat up and proceeded to slowly make our way toward the window. If this young lady had not moved her head there definitely was going to be a collision between my mirror and her face. Fortunately, she returned inside the window as we pulled up and began to look for the exact change in our wallets. At that moment, I noticed something unusual taking place that my friend was completely unaware of. As my friend was looking for exact change in the center console, he was completely unaware that she had moved her face and upper body out from the drive-thru window and literally into our car. She positioned her face about 18 inches from my friend's face. He still didn't know yet and I was definitely not going to tell him. He finally found that elusive penny and began to raise his head when suddenly he sensed her presence very close to him. In complete shock, my friend immediately leaned over the center console, into the back seat and erupted into hysterical laughter. I could not contain my emotions either. I had nowhere to go so I looked down to the floorboard and also erupted into laughter.

After probably only a few seconds, I looked up and realized that my friend was still in the back seat and had no intentions of coming back to the front. Then I made eye contact with the young lady.

Everything had changed at this point. She was back in the Arby's building with her hands on her hips and staring directly at me. Of course, my friend was still in the backseat, so who else could she look at. She said, "Are you laughing at me?" I began to calm my laughter and wiped the tears off of my face. I quickly replied, "Ma'am, if you don't mind me asking, why are you acting this way?"

Let's be honest, typically the answer to that question in the workplace is something like, "My boss is standing over there watching," "I'm a new employee" or "We just received this new training that tries to script the responses for our employees."

But her response was very different. Thankfully, her smile reappeared as she said, "I've never thought about it, but I guess I just love my job." Wow! What a statement! But honestly, at first, I missed it. I was so caught up in everything that had happened and had such anticipation of writing this account down in my journal that I missed the point. It was not until I heard the words "I just love my job," that I finally got it.

Love What You Do!

My dad had an adage for me growing up. He'd say, "Son, do what you love to do and you'll never work a day in your life." I discovered that love my freshman year in college. I loved to play golf. I took every chance I could to get to the golf course and play as many holes as possible. After playing for several years, I discovered that I still loved the game but also knew my dad's adage was difficult to fulfill. You see, I was not going to be able to make a living playing golf. After graduation and working for a few years, I continued to ask myself the question, "Am I doing what I love?"

That Saturday afternoon, an 18-year-old serving sandwiches at Arby's had no idea she had solved the difficulty with my dad's advice. The words are flipped! It's not, "Do what you love."

It's, "Love what you do!" Love what you do is possible; it's a choice. Over the years I've wondered if doing what you love is attainable for most people. Who you are now and where you are now is the time and place to do what you can to make a difference in your own life and lives of others around you. We often think to ourselves or tell others, someday things will be better, when I finish school, get the right job, meet the right person, live in the right city and the list goes on and on and on and on and on! That's the trap! I'm here now and I'll just wait it out until things change and then I'll be awesome. Be awesome now! The young lady at Arby's stood out because she chose to excel, to be awesome, no matter what she was doing. She made a choice that day to love what she was doing. Was it bizarre, funny, different? Well, of course, because it is so uncommon to see people flourish when they appear to be trapped. She was not trapped. She had escaped by simply choosing to be awesome where she was and as a result she had likely affected thousands by simply choosing to make a difference in the lives of others.

You Are Here. Here is Your Opportunity.

Take a few minutes to consider the following questions:

Who are you? _____

_____

_____

_____

_____

_____

_____

Where are you? _____

_____

_____

_____

_____

What can you influence? _____

_____

_____

_____

_____

_____

How can you step out of your trap and begin making a difference today? _____

_____

_____

_____

_____

_____

CHAPTER 5

Value Others.

By Kevin Tutt

VALUE OTHERS.

Ask a high-performing teacher, rafting guide, theme park employee or nurse, "What is the favorite part of your job?" The immediate answer likely will be, "Seeing success in others." It is our natural instinct to see those we value find success. Just ask the grumpiest, angriest person you know a question about his new grandchild and suddenly his entire mood changes. Why? Because people value their grandchildren. Suddenly you're hearing about the greatest child that has ever walked this earth.

We must understand that valuing the people we serve or live with is a key factor in our success. Unfortunately, we stumble into the complacency trap by simply focusing our attention on ourselves. You will not find value in all people, all day. It's not a realistic view of life. You can, however, seek opportunities to make a difference in a few lives each day.

Michael and I had just finished speaking together at Ashford University in Clinton, Iowa. As we raced back to Midway Airport in Chicago for a 5:30 p.m. Southwest Airline flight to Houston, Texas, a thunderstorm rolled in. We knew that our flight would be delayed and this became a major concern because we had three speaking engagements the following day in Texas. Three school districts would be hosting their teacher convocations the next day, and we were the keynote speakers. I was scheduled to speak twice in the Houston area, and Michael had a connecting flight to take him to Lubbock, where he would be speaking in the afternoon.

As we arrived at the gate, we were not surprised to see that our flight was delayed until 6:30 p.m. We weren't too concerned because we thought that would give us plenty of time to get to Texas and do what we needed to in preparation for the speaking engagements the next day. However, at 6:30 p.m., the schedule was moved again to 8:30 p.m. We began to panic.

As we followed the weather reports, we were aware that the storm had passed and the aircraft was at the gate. "So what's going on? Let's get this show on the road!" Then it changed again—10:30 p.m. "Are you kidding me?"

We became desperate to find a way back to Texas if the airline was going to let us down. We thought, "How about a rental car?" Nope, that would not work. It would be about 1,080 miles to Houston and around 16 hours of driving in a car. Reality was definitely setting in. "We have to get back to Texas!"

Finally at 10:30 p.m., we boarded the plane. We started to calm down and figure out solutions to make everything work. I would land in Houston, grab a hotel room for a few hours of sleep and I'd be rested enough to speak. Michael, on the other hand, would just have to gut it up. He would need to get a rental car in Houston for a one-way trip to Lubbock. He would drive all night and into the early morning and would be on campus, ready to speak at 1:30 p.m. Sure, Michael would get no sleep and would have to shower at a truck stop, but you have to do whatever it takes.

At midnight, our plane was still sitting at the gate. We had both fallen asleep, expecting to be awoken by the friendly sound of the flight attendant's voice explaining the safety instructions of this aircraft. Instead, we woke to the friendly sound of the pilot's voice saying, "This is your captain speaking. I apologize for the inconvenience, but Southwest Airlines has canceled all flights out of Midway Airport tonight. If you would please exit the plane and proceed to the ticket counter, we can get you all re-ticketed and we'll have you out of here first thing in the morning."

First thing in the morning! Somebody please tell me this is a dream and I haven't woken up yet. Michael and I were stunned. We knew there was absolutely no way we were going to be in Houston, Texas, by sunrise. There was no way that either one of us would be able to make our speaking engagements.

The next four and half hours were brutal. We literally lay on the floor in between taking slow, creeping steps toward the ticket counter. Hundreds of passengers from other flights also stood in line to be issued new tickets. We received a smile, an apology and a new itinerary for 4:30 a.m. As Michael and I annoyingly left the ticket counter to a get a coffee and a breakfast sandwich, we made a decision. We decided that we would never fly Southwest Airlines again. Our decision was based on three reasons. First, as we stood in line, a very positive and friendly flight attendant was there visiting with us. She explained that the storm had delayed so many flight that they were just not able to get caught back up and at midnight, all the pilots went "illegal," meaning they could not fly without rest. I completely understood and embraced this policy. My issue was that the plane sat at the gate for five and a half hours with no rain or storm.

Secondly, August is our busiest time of the year and three back-to-school speaking engagements were lost because of sitting at the gate for so long.

Thirdly, Michael and I had to call three school superintendents at 5:30 a.m. to let them know that we were stuck in Chicago and would not be able to speak at their kick-off.

As fate would have it, about six weeks later, Michael and I were speaking at a conference in Midland, Texas, that ended around 3:00 p.m. The next morning we were scheduled to speak at 8:30 a.m. in Corpus Christi, Texas, 470 miles away. Michael and I had made the decision to not drive so our only option was . . . you guessed it, Southwest Airlines. We both agreed this was the better option, despite our decision six weeks earlier.

Our flight from Midland to Corpus was again at 5:30 p.m. This time, there was no thunderstorm and we were able to arrive an hour early, as usual. We boarded the plane at exactly 5:30 p.m. and within minutes we were headed to Corpus Christi. As we settled back in the reclined position, we peeked at our itinerary and realized that we were scheduled to fly from Midland to Dallas, then to Houston, before finally arriving in Corpus.

The good news was that we were not going to have to change planes at each stop but there was an unloading and boarding of new passengers at each airport. The bad news was that our arrival time to our final destination was 10:45 p.m. Since Michael and I got to the airport at 4:30 p.m. and would not be getting to our destination until 10:45 p.m., we would not be able to eat dinner until well after 11:00 p.m.

As we landed in Dallas, the majority of the passengers exited and Michael and I were left on the plane considering how we would get food for survival. I was in the exit seat and Michael was against the window. After a 10 or15 minute wait, an extremely cheerful flight attendant stopped in the isle beside me and said, "Hey guys, we are about to begin letting the other passengers board, but before we do, is there anything special I could get you two?" Now, for a person like me that loves to keep a conversation going, I wasn't about to say, "No, we're good." Instead, I considered the likelihood of starvation if we had to wait so long for dinner and responded with, "That's a great question. A big burger combo would be awesome." She said, "That would be awesome, but unfortunately we don't have burgers on this flight. But when we land in Houston, there will be a Wendy's just outside the gate that we are coming into. You can definitely get your big burger combo there!"

As she turned to walk away, I launched out another question for her. I said, "Wait, wait, wait, wait. When we got on the plane, you kept our boarding passes. How do I just jump off to get burgers in Houston and then get back on the plane?" She looked at our itinerary and realized that we were going to continue on to Corpus Christi. She replied, "Oh, that's my mistake. I thought that Houston was your final destination. I see that you guys are headed on to Corpus and won't arrive until late tonight. I'm sorry. You can't get off the plane and back on. I see your dilemma here." Then she got real quiet, leaned over towards us both, slowly looked left and then right and whispered, "Here's what I'm going to do for you two guys. I'm going to set you up with an all-you-can-eat peanut buffet!"

Michael and I looked at each other smiling, acknowledging her creativity and wit. Given our hunger, we also were intrigued by what an all-you-can-eat peanut buffet might mean. The word buffet is always good to hear.

We had been in the air for about five minutes when I noticed our friendly flight attendant at the front of the plane with a monster bag of Southwest Airline peanuts. It was a clear plastic bag about two feet tall, filled with little packages of peanuts. Michael and I were sitting about six rows back from the front and I assumed she was taking this bag to the back of the plane to fill their little wicker baskets. But much to my surprise, she headed toward the back of the plane and when she got even with Michael and me, she looked like a quarterback running an option offense and pitched that bag of peanuts in our lap and then nonchalantly kept walking toward the back.

We were stunned. We grabbed that bag of peanuts like a couple of guys just rescued from a deserted island. She came back by with a "How's that for service?" look and asked what we might like to drink. We both ordered Dr Pepper, and right there two guys she had never met before in her life had an all-you-can-eat peanut buffet.

About 45 minutes later the captain said, "Please prepare the cabin for landing." Michael and I had eaten about a third of the bag. There had to have been about 400 packets of peanuts in there. I spun the bag up, and as she walked by I stopped her and said, "Here, take these before we get sick." She laughed and said, "I hope that holds you over until you can find somewhere to eat tonight. I did want to let you know that Houston is where I get off. There will be new flight attendants getting on board and they will take great care of you as you head on over to Corpus. And I just want to say that whatever it is that you two are doing tomorrow in Corpus, I hope you have a fantastic day and more importantly I hope you will always choose to fly Southwest Airlines."

Wow! What do you think my response was? Absolutely! Remember how this story started? Six weeks before, we were never going to fly Southwest again. The truth is that most of us can change our hard hearts just as easily. If someone would just take a little time to make us feel valued, we're back on board.

Just like she had told us, most of the passengers again exited the plane, as did the flight attendants. New flight attendants boarded the plane and began putting their luggage in the overhead bins. They got things ready for the next flight over to Corpus Christi.

Michael and I were sitting in our seats, still, feeling pretty special about the buffet dinner we just had. Then suddenly the new flight attendants began cheering for something. Michael and I looked up from our seats to try and see what was going on.

Here was the scene: the flight attendant that had provided us with the all-you-can-eat peanut buffet had reentered the plane and as she rounded the corner, into the cabin, she was walking towards us with a huge smile her face. I noticed that she had a Wendy's bag in one hand and a drink carrier in the other. I kid you not! Michael and I looked at each other and joined the other flight attendants in clapping, cheering and laughing. We were like kids on Christmas morning.

Just when we thought things couldn't get any better, they did! She sat the sack down on the tray table in front of me. I didn't hesitate before digging through the sack. Burgers, fries, ketchup . . . is this for real? And then the icing on the cake, I took a sip of my large drink. It was Dr Pepper. She remembered we loved Dr Pepper from our drink order during the flight. She was our hero! She had delivered exactly what we wanted because she paid attention to the details. We were stunned, just smiling and thinking, "I can't believe someone would do this!" The other flight attendants continued laughing and smiling and felt an amazing amount of pride. It was awesome to see them all celebrating one of their team members who had just experienced a "walk-off homerun." Game over. Because of her decision to go above and beyond, she won! We won! Southwest won!

From Selfish to Selfless

This story began with deciding we would never fly Southwest Airlines again. Months earlier we had felt cheated, as if no one cared about our schedule or the stress of disappointing three school districts. Then through a remarkable act of selflessness, we became Southwest's biggest fans. Mike and I felt as if we were the two most important people on the plane that evening. We felt valued!

So here's the trap. Often we become tired, numb to the world around us, and all we really want to do is get to the finish line. We feel that it's all we can do to take care of ourselves. We certainly don't have time to concern ourselves with others and their needs. We become comfortable in our decision to let what happens, happen. We forget we are in control and have the power to bring others with us. It would have been so simple for the flight attendant to simply look at Mike and me and say nothing. And by the way, that's what most of us have come to expect when it comes to a customer-service experience, nothing. But she didn't, she refused to stand in the trap of selfishness and drew us into the experience.

Show Value.

Identify the areas in your past where you added value to customers or others around you. _____

_____

_____

_____

_____

What caused you to stop valuing others? _____

_____

_____

_____

_____

What has stolen your passion for doing things differently?

_____

_____

_____

_____

Who can you value? _____

_____

_____

_____

_____

How can you value them? _____

_____

_____

_____

_____

Who do you need to take with you on life's journey? _____

_____

_____

_____

_____

CHAPTER 6

Have a Plan and Execute It.

By Michael Daggs

Have a Plan and Execute It.

Twenty-four hours. That's all any of us have in each day. One of the few things we all have in common is time. No one has more or less of it per day than anyone else. To escape the complacency trap, we must recognize that we will never have more time. That's not possible. Things will not be different, better, easier or more productive down the road. So what's the difference between those people who seem to get things done and those who run short of time?

A few years back, my family took a trip to Orlando, Florida. We were headed for our first visit to Disney World. My wife, Caroline, our son Lucas, who was four years old at that time, and I boarded a plane in Abilene, Texas, full of excitement and anticipation. All Lucas could talk about was the Buzz and Woody *Toy Story* character dolls that we had promised would be our first purchase when we arrived. Caroline had spent an enormous amount of time and effort to ensure that this trip would go off without a hitch. Somewhere thousands of feet over Alabama we flippantly made a huge error in judgment regarding our plans while at Disney World. Caroline and I made an executive decision that since we had devoted so much time and money to this trip, we were going to forgo any naps or rest breaks while we were at the "Wonderful World of Disney." Don't judge me! We didn't know!

We arrived and the first morning there, we woke early, ready to tackle the adventure of Disney World. Our first stop would be Magic Kingdom. Our first purchase would be the Buzz and Woody figures that we had promised Lucas. The morning truly was nothing short of magical. Lucas was strutting around the park with Buzz and Woody under each arm. Caroline was glowing, since everything was going exactly according to plan. And I, well, I was just loving the fact that my family was having so much fun.

Then the afternoon arrived and it happened. If you have ever been to Orlando in July you know exactly what happens in the afternoon. The natural sauna kicked on. Suddenly the heat mixed with thousands of people and the park became almost unbearable. But remember the executive decision? There will be no naps or rests breaks on this trip. So we continued to push on. At some point in the pushing on, it dawned on me that Lucas was no longer right beside me as he had been all morning. I immediately went into panic mode as I began looking all around for Lucas. It did not take long to find him. Lucas had simply stopped walking about 30 steps behind us. I walked backed to him and said, "What are you doing?" Lucas responded, as he choked back the tears, "I can't go anymore. I need you to take me back home." Mind you, he didn't say, "I need you to take me back to the hotel." He wanted to go home. How could this be?

I dropped to a knee and responded rather ineffectively by saying "Lucas, you've got to pull it together, son. We are at the happiest place in the world and you're crying." He responded back with another, "I just want to go home." I repeated, "You have got to pull it together. We've got to keep going until it gets dark." I realized that I didn't say anything all that motivating, but Lucas began forward movement again. But it was short lived.

About five minutes later, Lucas had shut down again. He stopped movement and repeated through his tears, "I just want to go home." It became obvious that we were not going to make it until dark. Desperate times call for desperate measures. I was also tired but I decided that I would pick Lucas up and put him on my shoulders. Sure, we had six more hours to go, but we had to keep pushing on.

It was a brutal afternoon for the family but we made it to 9:00 p.m. On our way out of the park, we were undeniably exhausted, sun burned, and extremely irritated with each other.

As I was walking down Main Street, USA, carrying my son, in front of Cinderella's castle, an enormous amount of people started pouring into the park. What could they possibly be doing? And why were they all in my way when all my family wanted to do was leave? Suddenly we realized what was happening. "Boom!" The sky lit up with a myriad of colors. As we turned around, we were amazed at the fireworks show that was taking place over Cinderella's castle. It was a glorious sight.

Though we were tired, angry and irritated from the experience of the previous six hours, that did not stop Caroline from saying, "You two, back up. We are getting a picture of this." That picture is still proudly in the photo album, tears and all.

The fireworks ended and we were finally headed for the exit with the strong desire to be back in our room, away from the events of that day. A few steps away from the exit, I began feeling pretty guilty for the way I had acted with my son, potentially ruining the magic of Disney for him. In efforts to make amends with Lucas, I bought him one of those metallic looking Mickey Mouse shaped balloons. Mickey seemed to at least wipe away some of the raw emotion of the trauma he had experienced that afternoon.

We boarded the shuttle and headed back to the room. Somewhere in route, Caroline looked at me and made a strong declaration. She said, "Tomorrow we are stopping after lunch and coming back to the room to rest." Those words seemed so profound, yet ever so elusive for us during that first day. But the new plan seemed to be the key to saving this trip.

We woke the next morning refreshed and ready to try again. We decided that we would leave everything in the room that day, including the Mickey Mouse balloon, Buzz and Woody. We would not be gone too long, for our plans were to be back in the room a little after lunch. The new plan was set and off we went.

The morning was great. With everyone still happy and pleasant around lunchtime, we rode the shuttle back to our room. Back at the hotel, we scaled the stairs that would take us to the walkway that led to our room. As we approached the room, we passed our window before we reached the door and something was clearly out of place. The metallic Mickey Mouse shaped balloon was in the little space between the curtain and window looking right at us, seemingly welcoming us back to the room. We could not help but laugh at the sight.

As I opened the door, Lucas darted in to the room ahead of us desperate to find his Buzz and Woody toys that he had left in the room. As I stepped into the room, instantly, I knew something was not right. We were greeted by very loud conversation. It was so loud that I assumed that someone was in our room and I began to look for the source of the noise. There wasn't actually anyone in our room. All the noise was coming from the television, which was on the Disney channel (of course) and turned to a very high volume. Upon seeing the television, Lucas began to holler for me.

He was standing behind us and between the two beds. He said, "Dad, look at the bed, look at the bed!" When I looked at his bed I was stunned. Buzz and Woody were propped up on the bed with some pillows and the covers were pulled half way up their bodies. A box of popcorn was sitting between them, two Pepsi's had been opened with straws sticking out of the cans and the television remote was sitting on Woody's lap. They appeared to be sitting on the bed, enjoying their favorite Disney show.

Lucas looked at me and exclaimed with unchecked excitement, "Dad, we ruined it! Before we came in here they were alive! They were alive!" That experience was nothing short of magical.

You've likely seen the movie *Toy Story*, or at least heard of the plot. Were Buzz and Woody really alive? Of course not. So, how did this amazing, magical moment take place? There was a young housekeeper who truly understood the opportunity that she had daily to positively affect the lives of others. She took the time not only to clean and reset our room for the day but also to exceed our expectations. We never met her and she never received special recognition for this effort. She simply decided to execute the plan. She worked hard and went the extra mile.

Occasionally, my family will get out the photo album of this trip and begin to scroll through the thousands of dollars, I mean, thousands of magical memories we had over those five days. But we always stop at that encounter and recall the moment that was created by someone we least expected it from.

Have a Plan.

To stay free from the time trap, you must have a plan. It can be long term or short term, but there must be a plan each day that directs you toward success. If you fail to plan, what will happen with your time during the day? Your day will simply control you. For example, if I have seven things to get done today and I plan my day around accomplishing these seven things, I feel in control of the day. If I have these same seven things to do but have not planned my day, anything that comes up will trap me into sliding things down the "to do" list. At the end of the day, I am frustrated and complaining that I simply don't have the time to get everything done. The fact is that's right. You can't possibly get everything done if you don't have a plan.

Execute the Plan.

Even if you've taken the time to establish a plan, you're not free from the time trap yet. You have to execute the plan. That day in Orlando, while my family and I enjoyed our time in the park, a young lady had a plan and more importantly understood how she would execute it. She had prepared for the day; she knew where the microwave popcorn was, had Pepsi and straws on hand. Her task for the day was to create magic. The plan for our room became easier when she saw the Buzz and Woody dolls. The execution fulfilled the plan and magic was created.

Don't Settle For Good Enough.

We often hear terms like cruise control, see what happens, cross that bridge when we get there, easy button. These all represent no plan, and with no plan there is no execution. You can probably think back to a time or situation in your life when you were passionate about something, but the leader, boss, owner, coach, teacher, whoever was not. They simply chose to do what had always been done and no longer had a plan for success. Here's the kicker. They certainly wanted to be successful and appeared to be working to be successful, but the reality of their failure lay within their having no real plan. Don't miss this! Execution was taking place every day. They were spending time doing something. But executing without plan leads to complacency, frustration and burn-out.

Time to Get Real

Has it ever crossed your mind that you have no plan? Are you simply a product of the day and the stimuli that bombard you daily? What is your plan and how well is it being executed in your personal and work life?

My personal plan: _____

_____

_____

_____

_____

_____

_____

How to execute this plan: _____

_____

_____

_____

_____

_____

_____

My work plan:_____

_____

_____

_____

_____

How to execute this plan: _____

_____

_____

_____

_____

CHAPTER 7

Stop Rationalizing.

By Kevin Tutt

Stop Rationalizing.

Eliminating excuses is the final key to escaping complacency. Excuses make complacency very comfortable and to a degree justify the good enough mentality. The unfortunate thing about excuses is how they eliminate the human will to overcome and push beyond our perceived abilities. This is true of our physical and mental abilities. The adventures of our lives can only be achieved by eliminating excuses and aiming for the top.

It was the second week in August and my daughter Kelsey's junior year of high school. We live in a small town in Texas where football is life. Football two-a-days had started. Cheerleaders were deep into sign painting, and parents were working hard to out-decorate all the other local school districts. It was Thursday night around 11:30 p.m. when my family headed for bed. Around 11:45 p.m., I heard my dogs barking. Our dogs have two kinds of barks. There is the "Hey, there's a varmint out there" bark, and then there's the "Hey, someone is in the driveway, potentially breaking into the house" bark. This was undeniably a "someone's at your house" bark.

I got out of bed, looked out my front door glass, and immediately knew what was going on. The full moon made it a pretty easy to see in the darkness, and I noticed several silhouettes running across my driveway. I ran back to my bedroom and slid my shoes on. My wife, Marci, said, "What's going on?" And I responded, "We're getting toilet-papered!" She jumped up and grabbed her shoes. As I came out of the bedroom, my daughters, Kelsey and Karson, were standing in the living room. They asked, "Why are the dogs barking?" Again I whispered, "We're getting toilet-papered!" They both took off to their rooms.

I am so pumped! We love when we catch someone papering our house. Because if we catch them, it's on!

I crept slowly to the front door and looked out again, in time to see a roll of toilet paper flying into the trees. I slung the door open and jetted out of the house. As the door opened, the posse of boys outside knew I had come out but didn't know where I had gone. The boys did the smart thing and began running down the road to where they had parked their trucks.

Allow me a moment to go back and set the stage. Two pickup truck loads of boys, all football players, juniors and seniors, had decided to decorate our house by throwing as much toilet paper as they could around the outside of the house and around the trees and shrubs. Where I am from, we call this getting TP'd.

The boys were all jogging back to their vehicles after they had seen the front door open and also saw me exit the house. However, they were unaware that I had maneuvered rather quickly and run up alongside a few of the slower boys. After a few strides, they realized that one of the boys running with them was actually me, and they screamed out, "He's here, he's here! Mr. Tutt is here!"

The entire group panicked and accelerated their speed of running. I saw the interior lights of their vehicles come on as some made it back to their truck. At that point, I was drenched in sweat because it was still about 90 degrees outside. I made a decision that if I could catch up with them, then I was going to be very unpredictable and jump into the back seat of one of the trucks.

As I reached one of the trucks, I grabbed the door jam and was in mid jump when I realized that some of these boys had made this TP activity a little more exciting than I had originally thought. Luckily I was able to somehow stop my momentum from jumping and landing in the middle of three guys sitting in the back of the truck. Not only did some of these boys think it would be fun to TP our house, but they had decided to do so while streaking!

As I was in mid jump into the back seat, a couple of them had horrified looks on their faces and scrambled to do their best to cover themselves with any available roll of toilet paper. I was able to correct my path and land on my feet outside the door. I looked at them as they struggled to find their clothes.

Fortunately, I diverted my attention back toward my house because I noticed my wife and two daughters running toward the action. I hollered, "Stop!" You can imagine their puzzled looks as I screamed.

Within a few seconds, all the boys were dressed and stood outside of the truck with very awkward looks on their faces. They quickly realized that I wasn't upset with them but rather laughing at them. We spent a few minutes laughing about the entire chase. The boys were glad that I wasn't angry. My wife was glad that we caught them before they were able to launch too many rolls of paper into the trees. And I was glad that my wife and daughters didn't see what the unused toilet paper was hiding.

My wife and I encouraged the boys to be careful and allowed them to head on their way toward more mischief. As they drove off, I asked Kelsey to text message one of the boys to find out where they were going next. He replied quickly with the name of the next victim while my family was making our way back to the house.

As we entered our home, we made an important family decision. We went straight to the pantry, grabbed a stash of water balloons and began filling them. I also grabbed a five-gallon bucket and we methodically placed the balloons so that they would not rupture during transport.

After filling about 20 balloons with water, we loaded into my pickup truck and headed toward the house where the boys were located. That particular house sits in a subdivision so it made it easy for us to get close to them without being spotted. We slipped up the block slowly in the truck. Our truck crept to a halt a few houses away. We exited and launched our first attack.

By pure destiny, our first water balloon made a perfect hit on the back of one of the boys. At this, the girls grabbed the entire bucket and charged! My three girls and I were throwing at any boy within sight and they were scattering like ants. It didn't take long to throw 20 balloons. As the two truckloads of boys left the scene, I heard one of them yell from a vehicle, "Tutt, this isn't over yet!"

My family sprinted back to my truck, realizing that our house was unprotected. We pulled into our driveway and found no sign of the boys. Kelsey texted one of the boys again. This time, he responded that his mom had said it was time for them to be done.

I'm no fool and I knew that with high school boys, they weren't going to get pelted with water balloons and then call it done. I knew, without a doubt, that they would be back. So we planned for the next attack. Marci and Kelsey unrolled a couple of water hoses and stretched them across our circle drive and got the spray nozzle ready for each hose.

Karson grabbed a box of Kleenex and a tub of flour. She then proceeded to lay out about 15 single ply Kleenexes on the counter and placed about a half cup of flour on each Kleenex. Next she pulled the four corners to the center and secured them with a piece of clear, scotch tape, creating the perfect "flour bomb." She swept them into an Easter basket that she found in the pantry and headed out the door.

Meantime, I ran into my bathroom and grabbed a new can of shave cream, removed the top, pushed the middle out of the top and placed it back on the can with duct tape. By removing the "foam" top off of a new can, it allowed the shave cream to spray about 10 to 15 feet. We were prepped and in position. Let the battle begin. It took only about 15 minutes before headlights began to appear in the distance. At 1:30 in the morning, both pickups full of boys were making their way toward our house and then the lights were cut.

Kelsey and Marci hid in some cedar trees around our drive, spray nozzles ready. Who has time to worry about rattlesnakes? I was crouched down beside the house, and I had no clue where Karson had gone.

Both trucks slowly turned into our driveway and the guys in the bed of the truck began throwing something toward our yard but I couldn't tell what it was. Finally, I discovered that they had gone back to the athletics field house at the high school and loaded two 50 gallon barrels of watermelon rind, left-over from the watermelon feast earlier that evening. They were pelting my porch with watermelon. After about a minute, Kelsey and Marci stormed out of the cedar bushes, spraying water and screaming at the top of their lungs. The boys then turned their aim toward my wife and daughter.

I was still laying low and then I saw him, the kid that probably had the original idea to do all this stuff. He was standing in the bed of the truck, so I took off in the dark, flew over the tailgate, wrapped him up and took him to the floor of the truck bed. I then began to cover him and the others nearby with shave cream. We battled for about two minutes, everyone was covered in sweat, water, shave cream and a little dirt and then all of a sudden, Karson appeared out of nowhere. Pow! She let the first flour bomb fly and it was a direct hit to me and the others I was battling. Then another and another and another flour bomb.

One important thing to know when using flour bombs is that they aren't a one and done device. They can be picked up and thrown until all of the flour has been knocked out of them.

Multiple flour bombs were being thrown, water was being sprayed and shave cream was being smeared from one person to another. After another five minutes, we called a cease-fire. Looking around, it looked like we had thrown pancake batter all over each other and my yard had exploded with watermelon. It was awesome!

It took only a few minutes to spray everyone clean with the water hoses. Marci told the boys that she had been texting some of their parents and it really was time for them to head home for the night. We huddled the boys up and told them thanks for making our night great, that we loved them and encouraged them to be careful going home.

A couple minutes later they were rolling out of our driveway and in a few more minutes my daughters' Facebook pages started blowing up. On social media, friends asked why we hadn't invited them to the party, parents were saying we were nuts and the guys were saying it was an awesome night.

Go All In, No Excuses.

So many times in life, we all have countless opportunities to go all in, to do something unexpected and create a memory for a lifetime. We all have chances to do things, say things or be things that we simply let pass us by because we think that it would take too much time or effort or perhaps no one would even care. That evening, around 11:45 p.m., I could have looked through the window, seen what was going on, stepped outside and yelled, "Hey, get outta here!" And that would have been the end. But by taking the opportunity to go for it, we created a memory that would last forever. We also built relationships with those who took the journey with us.

The Facebook post that meant the most to me was from a young man named Hunter. His post said, "Water wars with the Tutts, one of the best nights ever!" Hunter had lost his dad to cancer a couple of years earlier. If a few hours of lost sleep could get a young man to post that comment on social media, I have to believe it was worth it.

Perform Despite the Circumstances.

In 2004, I was serving as Director of Leadership and Organizational Development for Hendrick Health System in Abilene, Texas. The system was healthy in many ways, yet there were several opportunities for improvements, especially in terms of revenue, expenditures and employee morale. Once a month all members of the management team met on a Thursday morning for our "State of the Union" meeting. Tim Lancaster had become the new President/CEO in August 2004 and led the meetings. He and I had a terrific relationship and his drive for excellence had reignited my desire to be the best.

The meeting that morning began with an excellent devotional thought from Chaplin Bruce Lampert, and then Mr. Lancaster delivered a message that I believe changed the organization. He began by asking each of us to write down on a piece of paper, "What's wrong in your department, are you losing money, is staff turnover high and are you losing market share?" After several minutes of silence and the sound of writing, he began again. "If I were to ask each of you to read your paper, you all better have the answer to each of these questions. And if I asked you why, all of you would have excellent, valid excuses and reasons for the situation your department is currently in. But here's the deal. Stop rationalizing! Here's what I want to know. I don't doubt that these issues are real, but given the current circumstance of your department, what are you going to do about it?"

This question, I believe, was the springboard to massive change within the organization. Each director and manager was tasked with creating a plan and executing that plan immediately. We all needed more supplies, more staff, more clients, more doctors, more RNs. The fact was that wasn't going to happen. How can we become the best healthcare organization in the country with what we have? Let's spend our efforts more on winning and less on whining! That was the clear message. Several leaders were rescued from their traps of complacency while others chose to leave the organization. From 2004 to 2015, Hendrick Health System has become one of the most successful healthcare systems in the country. Feel free to visit their website for the complete history, national honors and expansion of services.

Avoid the Temptation to Rationalize.

Rationalization is a very comfortable trap to fall into. Often passion and commitment begin to fade when you think that you don't have the tools and means to be successful. There are literally hundreds of excuses and reasons for not stepping up or, in the case of my Thursday night TP war, stepping out. Let's face it, over-analysis, decision paralysis and doing nothing is much easier than going for it. Maybe it's time to get uncomfortable and ask yourself the question, given the circumstances, what are you going to do about it?

List the reasons you are not as successful as you would like to be:

_____

_____

_____

_____

_____

Given the circumstances, what is your plan to win with what you have? _____

_____

_____

_____

_____

About the Authors

Kevin Tutt

Kevin Tutt is one of the two creators of Tutt and Daggs, CPI. Kevin graduated from Texas State University and spent 12 years in the Healthcare Management and Organizational Development areas of the Hendrick Health System. He has taught undergraduate courses in health at Abilene Christian University.

Kevin has a straightforward and humorous presentation style that is loved by audiences of all types. His sincere approach to improvement causes participants to apply presentation information to their own lives. Kevin inspires his audiences to exceed expectations and maximize their potential.

Kevin and his wife, Marci, have been married 28 years and have two daughters, Kelsey and Karson. Kevin loves being at the lake, fishing and traveling to Colorado.

Michael Daggs

Michael Daggs is the other brilliant mind behind the development of Tutt and Daggs, CPI. Prior to working at Hendrick Health System, where he met Kevin Tutt, Michael served as the Community Educator at Scott and White Hospital. Michael then served nine years in Healthcare Management and the Organizational Development and Efficiency departments at Hendrick Health System. He has taught undergraduate courses in health at Abilene Christian University.

Michael's obvious passion for life and excellence and his experience as a presenter give him a unique ability to quickly engage audiences and deliver powerful presentations that are easily applied.

Michael is a graduate of Hardin-Simmons University. He has been married 18 years to his lovely wife, Caroline. They have two children, Lauren and Lucas. They love spending time together as a family. Michael also loves outdoor adventures, golf and coaching his kids' sports teams.

CPSIA information can be obtained at www.ICGtesting.com
Printed in the USA
BVOW08s1912080416

443439BV00001B/3/P